SINFUL BUT NOT FORSAKEN.

A SERMON,

PREACHED IN THE

PRESBYTERIAN CHURCH, FIFTH AVENUE AND NINETEENTH STREET, NEW YORK,

ON THE

DAY OF NATIONAL FASTING,

JANUARY 4, 1861.

BY

ALEXANDER T. McGILL,

OF PRINCETON, NEW JERSEY.

[PUBLISHED BY THE CONGREGATION.]

NEW YORK:
JOHN F. TROW, PRINTER, 50 GREENE STREET.
1861.

SERMON.

"For Israel hath not been forsaken nor Judah of his God, of the Lord of hosts; though their land was filled with sin against the Holy One of Israel."—JEREMIAH, li. 5.

To be all but gone is a condition of despair to any man but a Christian. While there is nothing more than the conviction of sin against the Holy One of Israel, men of the world will have their hopes; and because sentence against an evil work is not executed speedily, their hearts are fully set in them to do evil. But when judgments are actually upon them, and calamity comes to be realized, they "are at their wit's end," their hands hang down in the weakness of dismay. They have not courage to stand "between the dead and the living," or go down to the bottom of deep distress, with nothing but a confiding hope that they are not wholly forsaken of God. This belongs only to the man who has God for "his God," and knows him to be "the Lord of hosts." It is not for us to despair, when we see no possibility of relief in visible expedients.

When Charles V. imperiously required the Confession of Augsburg to be abandoned, and gave the Protestant leaders only six months more in which to make up their minds finally, the cause of the Reformation was thought to be hopeless. But Luther exclaimed, "I saw a sign in the heavens, as I looked out of my window at night—the stars, the hosts of heaven held up in a vault above me; and yet I could see no pillars on which the Master had made it to rest. But I had no fear it would fall. Some men look about for the pillars, and would fain touch them with their hands, as if afraid the sky would fall. Poor souls! Is not God always there?" The pillars of our vault so beautifully starred below the heavens, our Federal arch, are falling, and the arch itself is breaking, and all expedients to prop and restore it have utterly failed. And now, the great question in this extremity of peril is, where is our God? We are sure he is angry with us; our sin has found us out. But is he gone forever? Are we now "forsaken," as a widow is left when her husband, or an orphan is left when her father, is dead? —the true force of the term in our text. He hath said to nations, if ye forsake me I will forsake you; and we are met this day to try our ways, and see how far we have forsaken him. However unlike our circumstances in most respects may be, to those of Israel and Judah when this prophecy was uttered, there are four particulars, in which they appear to be strikingly similar:

1st. Our land is full of sin against the Holy One of Israel.

2d. The punishment of sin is already upon us.

3d. There is evidence to believe that God has not forsaken us yet.

4th. He is our only help and hope in such a crisis.

I. The proprieties of a national humiliation before the God of our fathers, lead me to mention only such sins as this whole nation should deplore with ingenuous contrition. Not sins, however, my Brethren, which belong to the nation, and not to ourselves individually: it is even mainly because we have sinned as individuals, that God is filling us now with consternation and sorrow.

(1) Consider then, in the first place, that we are a nation of "boasters." There is not one of us, probably, whose soul has not been lifted up with pride for the greatness of our country, in every particular, which constitutes true national grandeur.

Her traditions, her immunities, her extent of territory, her advancement in resources of moral and intellectual power, as well as material greatness, have filled her sons and daughters everywhere, and especially when abroad, with inexpressible pride and exultation.

Our fathers would have looked on these things with gratitude, more than pride. If there was one feeling more than another, like a Christian grace, which predominated in the breasts of those who framed our Constitution, it was humility. With trembling solicitude, they started what they knew to be an experiment, which the world had never witnessed before; except in the solitary model of the Hebrew commonwealth, which first gave the hint of a mixed general and state or tribal government. Although their excessive jealousy of a state religion led them, in the opposite extreme of shunning theocratic forms, to adopt a Constitution which might be the political creed of an atheist as well as a Christian (for which, perhaps, God is angry with us till this day), still they did their work with humbleness of mind. And if, instead of leaning on the work of their hands, more than we lean on God our maker, if, instead of blazoning on every page of our national literature, pæans to the immortal instrument of our liberties and glory, we had retained the same humility, and watched over it with the meekness and fear in which it originated, we would not this day be covered with the shame and confusion of a stupendous failure. God will not give his glory to another, neither his praise to graven images. Though graven upon eternal brass, our Constitution were not better than the idols he abhors, when we lavish upon it the incense of such vainglorious devotion. And it is a marvellous way with the Almighty, in punishing boasters, to do it suddenly. In one hour a king of kings was changed, from a vaunting monarch to a grazing beast, for the proud boast: "Is not this great Babylon, that I have built for the house of the kingdom, by the might of my power, and for the honor of my majesty?"

Let us not reckon this sin to be a little one, comparatively venial on the catalogue of sins, to be acknowledged this day. See it, where the spirit of inspiration has enrolled it, along with the darkest crimes that belong to any degenerate age. Rom. i. 29–32; also 2 Tim. iii. 1–5.

(2) Prominently given in both these catalogues, is the *second* sin I mention, for which we should be humiliated as a people—*covetousness.* "For the iniquity of his covetousness was I wroth, and smote him: I hid me, and was wroth, and he went

on frowardly in the way of his heart." It is said our plan of union would hardly have been adopted at all, but for the clamor of material interests. The utter confusion of commerce and finance under the old confederation, and the incurable uncertainty of markets and exchange, without a common rule, constrained many, who were otherwise opposed to the experiment, to try it—venturing, as they supposed, a political peril, for the protection by a common flag, of our sails on every sea, and our citizens in every corner of the earth. But who does not know that this common security has proved a snare to the souls of men, and made our nation a proverb of greed over all the world? He who would have us let our moderation be known to all men, and tells us that covetousness is idolatry; and they "who will be rich fall into temptation and a snare, and into many foolish and hurtful lusts, which drown men in destruction and perdition;" who has added to these admonitions of his word, many a signal warning in his providence—sending panic after panic, even while the world was coming to buy our cotton, our grain, and our gold; and who has so often made us feel the very same insecurity we had escaped, in the fluctuating policy of the Government we adored, now at length says, in the thunder of his wrath,

" In vain have I smitten your children, they receive no correction."

I speak not of enormous and fraudulent grasping for money; the shameless corruption which seems to reign at the Federal capitol, and every State capitol of the Union; the astounding defalcations that make the ears of men to tingle—betraying such a loss of public virtue, as itself to incur the avenging displeasure of God upon the nation; but that inordinate love of the world, which prevails even among the people of God, rich and poor—the love of money for its own sake, and for the sake of pleasures in the world, that "nourish their hearts as for the day of slaughter."

(3) The bands with which we flattered ourselves the Union was being indissolubly bound together, have been made offensive to the Holy One of Israel. The rivers and the railroads were thought to be like arteries and veins in the human body, which would bring the people of every terminus more and more to beat with kindred feeling and a common interest. But these thoroughfares have been made by man's cupidity to break the laws of God; to profane his holy Sabbath; to cheat each other in a ruinous competition; and to rob the country at large—thousands of poor men, whose investments have been sunk, by guilty recklessness and actual fraud. With all

the honorable exceptions that should be made, the land is filled with sin by the very spread of enterprises, which go to make one brotherhood of the nation.

(4) It is filled with sinful abuse of rulers. "Thou shalt not revile the gods, nor curse the ruler of thy people." No matter who it is that holds the reins of government at Washington, in every political agitation, the land is full of maledictions upon him. And never, perhaps, were these so bitter and insulting as at present. Yet he is the minister of God to us, who beareth the sword by the ordinance of Heaven, whose venerable name should be guarded from contempt, in the arms of "supplications, prayers, intercessions, and giving of thanks," according to the divine exhortation. How many even of God's own people, in this day of rebuke and blasphemy, have reason to deplore the idle words and unclean lips, with which they have sinned in this thing against the Holy One of Israel!

Even if our President were the most perfect man that ever sat upon the chair of Washington, for wisdom and patriotism, decision and courage, the tempest of execration upon him of late is enough to make the strong man reel and stagger; to provoke Almighty God to take his understanding from him, and make our chief ruler a child; in order to punish the "frowardness" of a cursing republic. I have long feared, that for this iniquity alone, in which we have a bad preëminence, we should become a by-word among the nations, and suffer the terrible retribution, which the Bible approves: "As he clothed himself with cursing like as with a garment, so let it come into his bowels like water, and like oil into his bones."

(5) The land is full of sins in the *family government;* that holy and happy institute, which underlies all social order, and integrity of the commonwealth. The nurseries of piety and fraternal love, from which every tree that gives either fruit or shade must be transplanted to the State, have become hotbeds of political ambition. Time was, when the most animating topics of conversation at the fireside were lessons in the Bible and the catechism, the pastor's sermon, the missionary's letter, and the weekly journal, with its summary of important events. But now the newspaper, morning, noon, and night; the newspaper, with the returns of some election, or the virulent dissection of some political candidate; the newspaper, with its depraved insinuations and its incendiary lies, to inflame the wicked passions of the soul—is the pabulum of covenanted households, week-day and Sabbath. Boys are politicians. Public life is a game they are taught from infancy to

play without heart or conscience; the universal trade, in which nothing is at a discount so much as the capital of true patriotism and consistent integrity. From the cradle to the grave our people now talk politics. No wonder God comes down to curse a Babel like this, with confusion of counsels and tongues. No wonder fanaticism has left the cloisters of religious bigotry to seize on politicians, North and South, East and West, until it now rides on the whirlwind of passions, which have had a life-long ferment in the animosities of party.

But where could the catalogue end of specialties in sins, which may be fairly charged upon all the people of all sections, who are called this day to fasting and supplication? And when we consider that each section has its own peculiar iniquities, for which to be humbled, and that every State apart, and every city apart, and every family apart, and every individual apart, has other specialties to be cast into the fearful aggregate; and not the multitude only, but the magnitude also of our iniquities, each trespass by itself "grown to the heavens," by reason of aggravations in the abuse of light, and liberty, and warnings, and forbearance,—O! how should we "abhor ourselves and repent in dust and ashes!"

II. The punishment of our sin is actually upon

us. So the text intimates in the original force of the term, and so we feel in the sad realities, which this day fill us with grief and dreadful apprehension. Every flash of the telegraph is bringing new tidings of peril and disaster. The most fixed and trusting of God's children seem to be "afraid of evil tidings." Never was judgment so swift of foot against the sins of any nation. Centuries are days. The gradual decay of nations with which we are familiar in the traditions of the past, working with its bane through many long generations, and covering with a flush of health the body politic, while disease is on the vitals, is not the way of death decreed to this gigantic empire. Three months ago, we were counted over all the earth as the most favored of nations. Hitherto incredulous men that glory in the yoke of hereditary power, were talking, in view of the crisis at hand (our Presidential election), about the well-known elasticity of this fabric; how it had so often withstood commotions of the people, and was wont to settle down more firmly than ever, from the agitations with which it had been tossed. But, alas!—how changed—"our glorious beauty is a fading flower!" Secession—angry secession—bloody secession—all the horrors of a fratricidal war have made bare the arm. And not in sudden frenzy, or by mistake, which has roused to fury unwonted passions; but it seems, that wrath, long brooded, sullen, and reserved, proclaims the unalterable purpose—by right of self-preservation, and by the obligations of a sacred trust committed to its keeping by Almighty God—to dash this Government to pieces! Fanaticism from the North, and fanaticism from the South, seem now at length to be left alone upon the field; and a fight like theirs must be eternal. Only the Father of eternity can be our help and hope in such a crisis; and let us turn from the dark picture before us, to see what evidence we have, that he has not wholly forsaken us.

III. (1) We have not yet been filled with that inveteracy of sin, for which Israel and Judah were ultimately cast off from the Lord, as we have it described by his apostle, 1 Thess. ii. 15. The great heart of the American people, sinful as it may be, revolts alike from the punishment upon us, and its proximate causes on every side. And could we but look away from the confusion of politicians, to the deep yearning of millions, who have too long intrusted their common weal to men of selfish ambition, and hear the great constituencies which make up the heritage of God in our land, say to the man of conscience and unostentatious talents, 'the post of honor is no longer in a private station—the Lord hath need of thee to guide the counsels of the country; and these obstinate, corrupt, and designing demagogues that have brought our country to the brink of ruin, must be discarded forever,'—then might we hope, even yet, that the breach already made is not "wide as the sea," and that we can all live together, as brethren, "quiet and peaceable lives in all godliness and honesty."

(2) Family ties and friendships, bands of consanguinity and affinity, remain between the North and the South, to draw, with cords of love, the alienated sections together. These delicate tendrils seem indeed to be nothing now, in the tempest of passion. But they will be entwined to a mighty cord, when reason is allowed to resume her throne, and the irrepressible instincts of Christian civilization gather back the force, to which political rage has always submitted.

(3) One church is yet undivided. Though great andpopular churches of the land have led in this work of sectional strife, and anticipated the country in the folly of disunion, and much responsibility for the calamities we mourn may be resting on the heads of ecclesiastics, one church remains; in more than nominal union, a union of heart and

soul, though sadly pained this day at the rash and inflammatory utterances within her of eloquent tongues. I believe the union of States might crumble into fragments, and the Old School Presbyterian Church would not be dismembered. A very slender filament, you say, to span a gulf already made, and widening every hour: the surges already in the breach are too violent for any common interest to live. But remember, that if this bond remain at all, it must be, as it has been for a century and more, on grounds of intelligent comprehension of the whole question at issue, and therefore on grounds quite sufficient to bring the country together in abiding peace. Who knows but that it may be the glorious mission of the Presbyterian Church, in these last and perilous days, to wipe out the scandal which has rested on visible Christianity ever since the days of the apostles; and instead of civil power interposing to heal divisions in the Church, the Church will come, with plastic hand, to bind a shattered confederacy in better union than ever?

(4.) The revivals of religion over all our land, so recent, prove that God has not forsaken us—that "God in the midst of us is mighty; he will save; he will joy over us with joy; he will rest in his love, and joy over us with singing." True, indeed, ever since the day of Pentecost prepared the Church for her martyr age, a great baptism of the Holy Ghost has often been precursor to a baptism of blood, upon the Church and the country. The great awakening of the last century, under the ministry of Whitfield, Edwards, the Tennents, and others, which filled the land with so many converts of righteousness, came like a harbinger, to prepare the American people for long and gloomy wars; war with the French and the Indians, and war with the mother country herself, in our hard Revolution. A great revival in the early years of this century, in which the whole country shared, and especially that region which had been most insurgent under the first trial of our government, came in mercy to prepare the country for the war of 1812; in which our whole fabric was terribly shaken, by intestine conflicts, as well as outward foes; when the liberty of the press was put down by mobs, and a distinguished soldier of the Revolution was murdered by the populace of Baltimore, in a prison. That was a time when the sages of the land were despondent, as they are now, for the ultimate success and integrity of this Government.

What, then, if even the worst period of our eventful history be now upon us, and tribulation such as the land has never seen, be now at hand, for "the trial of the innocent," as well as punishment of the guilty, in a common desolation? These intimations may assure us, that God means to stand by us, and that "the Hope of Israel and Saviour thereof in time of trouble," is not standing by us only "as a stranger in the land, and as a wayfaring man that turneth aside to tarry for a night."

(5) The conspicuous instrumentality, which "the Lord of hosts" has been shaping for his own ends, in the progress of the Gospel and redemption of the world. Two great nations, the freest on earth, speaking a common language, and promulging a common faith, on opposite hemispheres, are confederates in the hand of our enthroned Messiah, for the salvation of men. Lately, the treasures of the earth were put into their hands, by remarkable discoveries, about the same time; and along with this magnificent inheritance to each, international jealousies have changed to confidence and kindness, and a feeling of friendship, which at this moment is a fervent flame. Think you, that one of these powers will now be taken, and the other left, in the work of the world's regeneration? That the older one is destined to advance with the high commission upon her, while the younger one expires in the convulsions of a day? That the mother must outlive the daughter; and an empire, on which the sun

can never set, may defy dismemberment, while we are failing to belt a single continent with our civilization? No: I cannot think it. Remember how the English empire had nearly fallen to pieces, but three years ago, and the world pronounced her Asiatic domination at end. Yet God preserved it; coming as the Lord of hosts, in the darkest hour of her extremity, because he had not forsaken her. And will he not be quite as sure to come for our help, and preserve her ally here, with unbroken energies for the same great end—millennial peace and glory to a ruined world?

(6) God has not forsaken us, because we are here with him, in his sanctuary this day, invited by his own word, and led by his own providence, to humble ourselves, just where "he waiteth to be gracious." Political sanctions from opposite sources, your President and your Governor, with one voice commend the act of this humiliation. "Our God" will never disappoint the hope he has himself excited; he never moves the hearts of men to bow in common contrition, without an answer of peace and an interposition of mercy. Yet, however sure we are, that it is good for us to draw nigh unto God, we may not be sure, that the specialty of deliver ance we crave is the best form for us, in which our prayer may be answered. Let it now suffice,

IV. That He is our only help and hope. "Should not a people seek unto their God?" All refuge else has failed. Vain is the help of man. His best devices only aggravate disorder, and make the alienation more incurable. The destiny of our "delightsome land" no sagacity of man foresees—never was the futurity of a nation so impenetrable. We are balancing on the finger of infinite sovereignty. We deserve the worst; we hope for the best. All that we can see and know is, that our God has not forsaken us, and that he is "the Lord of hosts"—that if he will deign to grant our literal request, all impossibilities vanish. "The stars in their courses fight against Sisera." But if not, we know that God himself is a refuge, "an hiding place from the wind, and a covert from the tempest." If he is with us as individuals, as families, and as churches, then may confederacies be dissolved, and all the foundations of the earth be out of course; but leaning on his almighty arm we go up from the wilderness, happy and safe.

The sovereignty of grace and the sovereignty of power, which the Holy One of Israel expresses on the face of my text, are "the two immutable things," to which we must fly for strong consolation, in this hour of trouble. Close in with the first, and the second will be sure to give you repose and satisfaction, whatever befalls us. You know perhaps already, what it is to lie at the feet of sovereign power, adoring it as good, even when it has torn from your embrace the dearest creatures on his footstool, because you feel that sovereign grace is yours in covenant, and better to you than the universe besides. In such posture of the soul it is, that we must bow to the good pleasure of the Most High, as we leave in his hand the destiny of our beloved country. If he will be pleased to give us back our union, and peace, and mutual affection, we shall adore him; and "in the name of our God we will set up our banners." But if he will suffer man to prevail, with the desolating fury of his passions, and the axes of angry infatuation, to break down the carved work of our beautiful edifice, then "a glorious high throne from the beginning is the place of our sanctuary;" and we turn to it with full assurance of protection and repose: "Come, my people, enter thou into thy chambers, and shut thy doors about thee; hide thyself as it were for a little moment, until the indignation be overpast."

"When, in the time of the Judges, the children of Israel gave themselves up in a shameless manner to the worship of idols, they fell under the wrath of God, and were eighteen years oppressed by the Ammonites and Philistines. Still, when they came to themselves, and cried to the Lord, they joined to their repentance lowly submission, and said, 'We have sinned: do thou unto us whatsoever seemeth good unto thee.' This is the temper which sanctified affliction always begets, so that the prostrate soul dares no longer to impose terms on Jehovah, but yields itself to his sovereign discretion. There is peace in such surrender, a peace which is altogether independent of any expected mitigation of the stroke."* These are the words of one who was a great link between the North and the South; whose voice would have been more potent in the din of this confusion, than that of any minister who survives him; but whom his Master, in mercy to him, took away from the evil to come. And may we all, with "like precious faith," when our work is done, be gathered to the same happy home; where "the days of our mourning shall be ended" —where sin and sorrow can reach us no more—where "the wicked cease from troubling, and the weary are at rest."

* Alexander on Consolation, p. 231

www.ingramcontent.com/pod-product-compliance
Lightning Source LLC
LaVergne TN
LVHW011147110826
845150LV00008B/2553
* 9 7 8 1 4 1 8 1 9 1 9 3 1 *